Gateway Arch

Lori Dittmer

Creative Education • Creative Paperbacks

Road map of Contents

4 Welcome to the Gateway Arch!

9 Designing the Gateway

13 Strong Legs

16 Visit the Gateway Arch

20
Activity:
Make an Arch

22
Glossary

23
Read More
& Websites

24
Index

Welcome to the Gateway Arch! This **monument** sits near the Mississippi River in St. Louis, Missouri.

Reaching 630 feet (192 m) high, the Arch is the tallest human-made monument in the United States. It is part of Gateway Arch National Park.

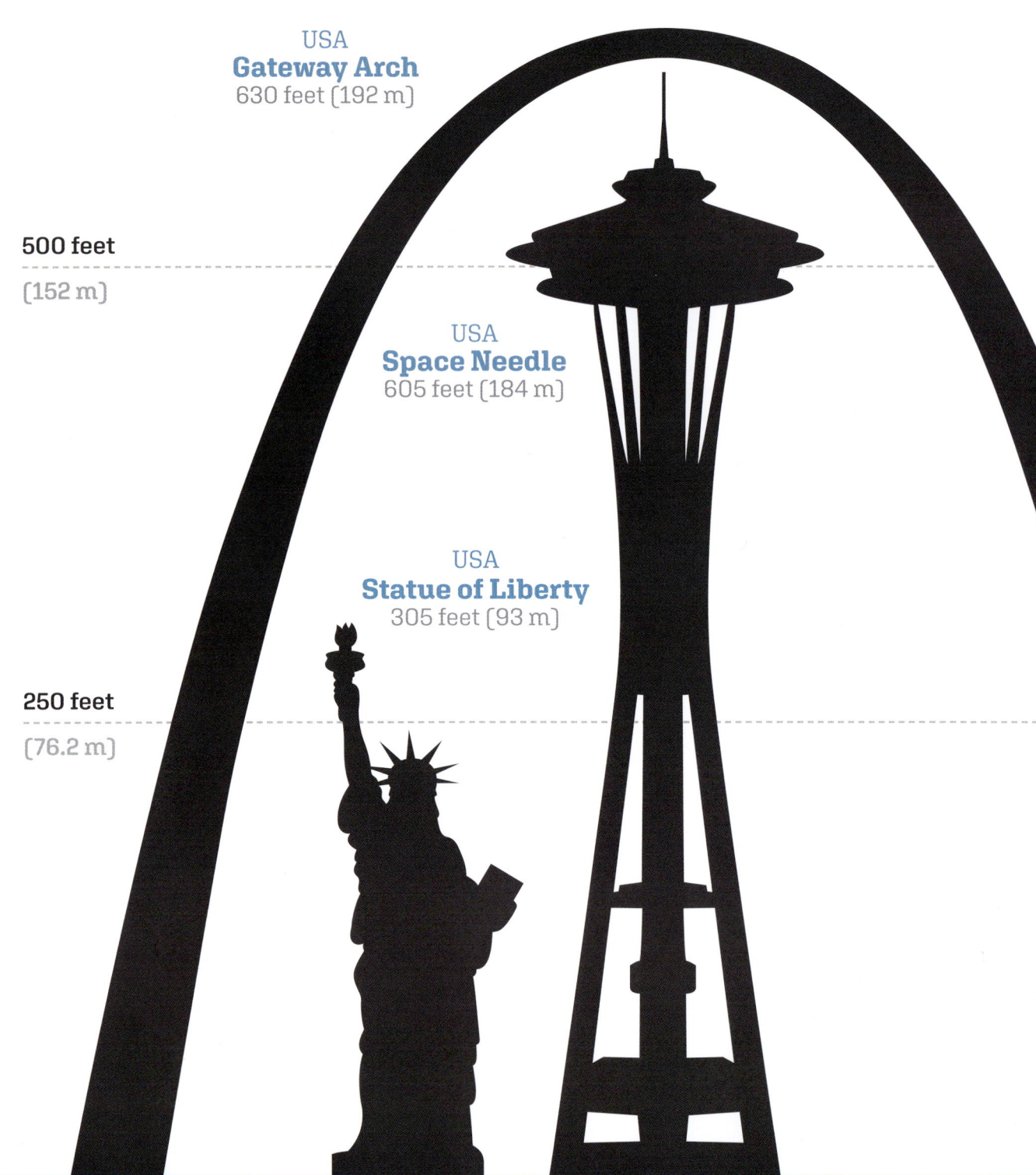

How tall is the Gateway Arch?

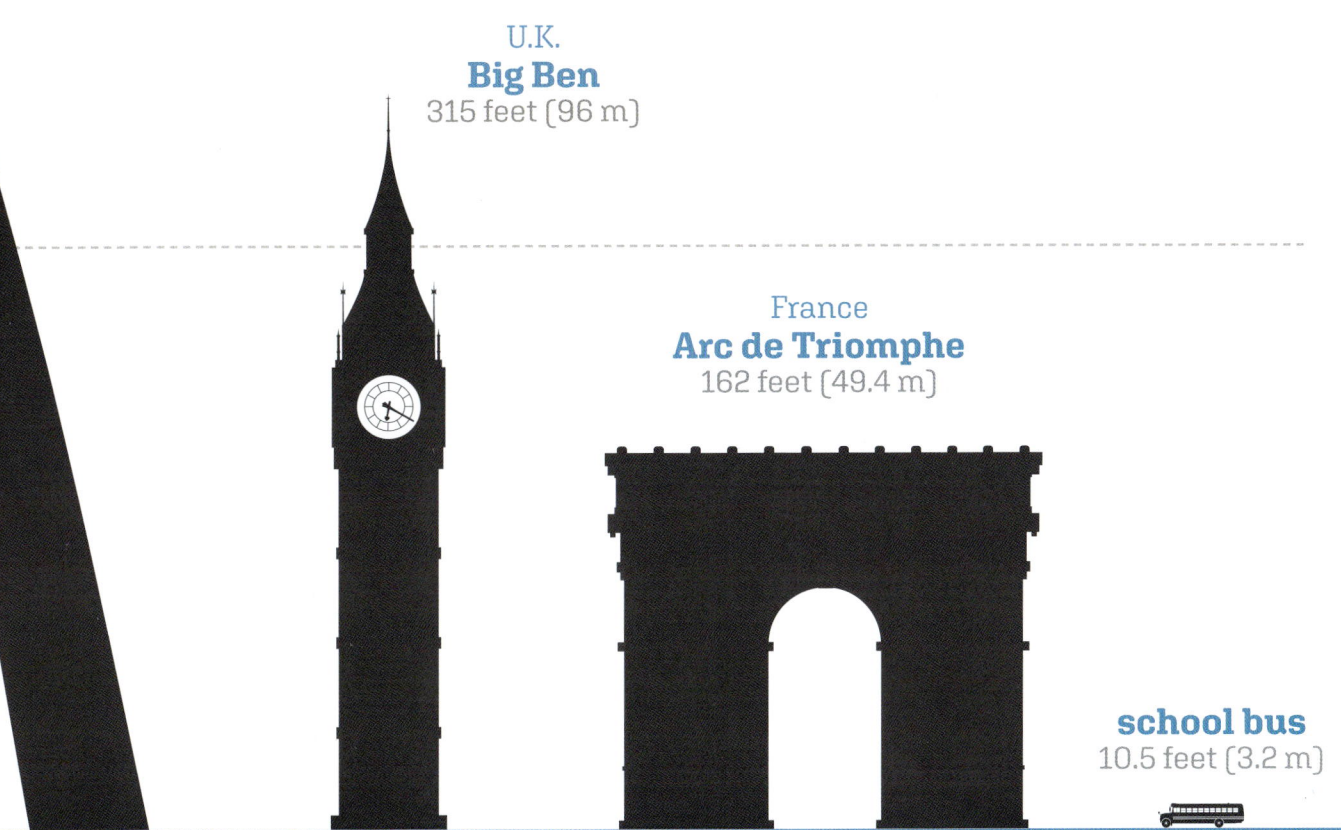

U.K.
Big Ben
315 feet (96 m)

France
Arc de Triomphe
162 feet (49.4 m)

school bus
10.5 feet (3.2 m)

St. Louis is known as the "Gateway to the West." During the 1800s, thousands of **pioneers** ventured into the western part of the country. Many set out from St. Louis. In the 1930s, the government decided to build a **memorial** to honor them.

Designing the Gateway 9

Eero Saarinen won a contest to design the memorial. His drawing featured a large metal arch. Construction began in February 1963. It was finished in October 1965. Afterward, workers added a **tram** inside the Arch.

◄ Eero Saarinen

Designing the Gateway 11

Builders made the Arch from steel and concrete. They started at the bottom. The legs are 630 feet (192 m) apart at the base. A truss kept the legs stable near the top. Then workers added the last section. The foundations for the legs are solid concrete. They go 60 feet (18.3 m) down into the ground.

Strong Legs

150
Can withstand mph winds

18
Can sway inches in either direction

60
Foundations reach feet into the ground

The Arch sways slightly in strong winds. It was built to withstand earthquakes. During a 1968 tremor, it shook for 40 seconds.

Millions of people visit the Gateway Arch each year. If you go, ride the tram to the top. Look out the windows in the viewing area. On a clear day, you might be able to see for 30 miles (48.3 km)!

Can you spot these in the picture above?

Old Courthouse

Busch Stadium

Museum of Westward Expansion

Afterward, visit the museum beneath the monument. If you have time, take a riverboat cruise on the Mississippi. Enjoy the view of the Arch from the river!

Visit the Gateway Arch

★ **Activity** ★

Make an Arch

------------------ materials ------------------

cardboard
a piece about 6 inches (15.2 cm) long on each side

string
12 inches (30.5 cm) long

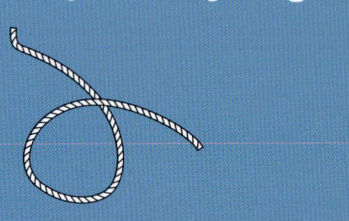

all-purpose glue

scissors

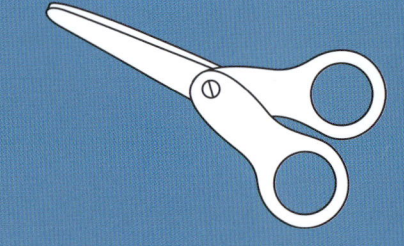

tape

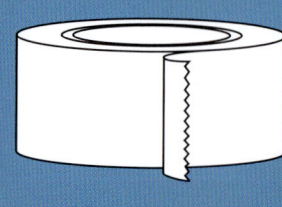

Cut a slit on opposite sides of the cardboard. Slide string into slits, taping the ends.

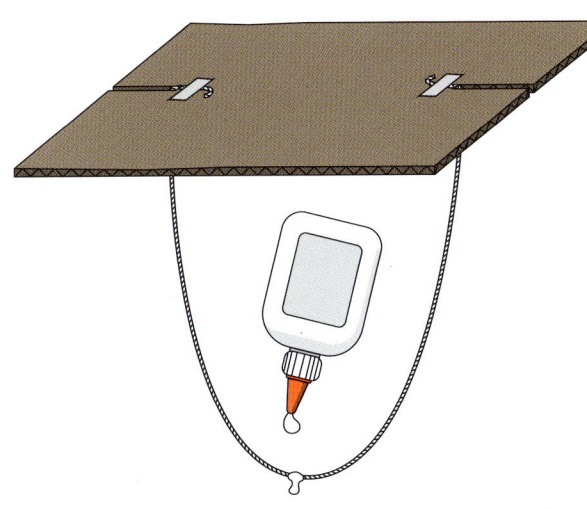

Hang the cardboard upside down (between two desks, for example). Coat the curved string with glue.

Let dry overnight. Then flip over the cardboard. You have made an arch!

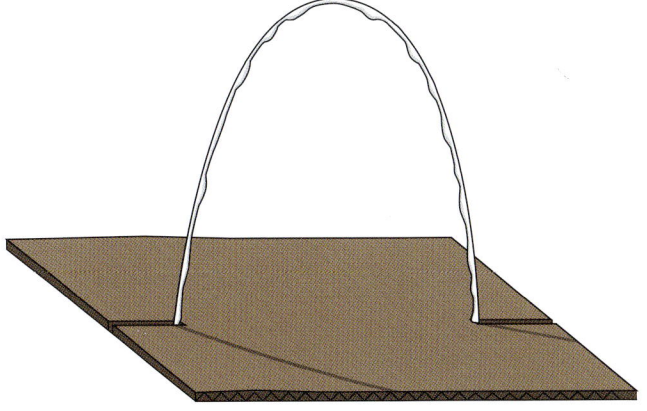

Glossary

foundations
the lowest weight-bearing parts of a structure

memorial
something that reminds people of a person or event

monument
a structure built to honor a person or event

pioneers
the first people to explore and settle in a region

tram
a passenger car that runs on cables or tracks

truss
a framework of beams or bars

Read More

Marsh, Carole. *I'm Reading About the Gateway Arch*. Peachtree City, Ga.: Gallopade, 2016.

Mattern, Joanne. *The Gateway Arch: Celebrating Western Expansion*. South Egremont, Mass.: Red Chair Press, 2018.

Websites

National Park Service: Kids & Youth- Gateway Arch National Park

Learn about the history of the Gateway Arch, and print out an activity sheet.

https://www.nps.gov/jeff/learn/kidsyouth/index.htm

Wonderopolis: How Was the St. Louis Arch Built?

Read more about the Arch, and watch a video to see it from the air.

https://wonderopolis.org/wonder/how-was-the-st-louis-arch-built

Note: Every effort has been made to ensure that the websites listed above are suitable for children, that they have educational value, and that they contain no inappropriate material. However, because of the nature of the Internet, it is impossible to guarantee that these sites will remain active indefinitely or that their contents will not be altered.

Index

construction	11, 13	Mississippi River	4, 19
features	4, 11, 13, 15, 16	Saarinen, Eero	11
Gateway Arch National Park	4, 19	St. Louis, Missouri	4, 9
		visitors	16, 19

PUBLISHED BY CREATIVE EDUCATION AND CREATIVE PAPERBACKS
P.O. Box 227, Mankato, Minnesota 56002
Creative Education and Creative Paperbacks are imprints of The Creative Company
www.thecreativecompany.us

LIBRARY OF CONGRESS CATALOGING-IN-PUBLICATION DATA
Names: Dittmer, Lori, author.
Title: The Gateway Arch / Lori Dittmer.
Series: Landmarks of America.
Includes bibliographical references and index.
Summary: Examining the building process from the ground up, this high-interest title covers the history and construction of the Gateway Arch, one of Missouri's most well-known landmarks.

Identifiers: LCCN: 2018061062
ISBN 978-1-64026-124-2 (hardcover)
ISBN 978-1-62832-687-1 (pbk)
ISBN 978-1-64000-242-5 (eBook)

Subjects: LCSH: Gateway Arch (Saint Louis, Mo.)—Juvenile literature. / Gateway Arch (Saint Louis, Mo.)—Study and teaching (Elementary)—Activity programs. / Saint Louis (Mo.)—Buildings, structures, etc.—Juvenile literature.
Classification: LCC TA660.A7 D57 2019
DDC 721/.41—dc23

COPYRIGHT © 2020 CREATIVE EDUCATION, CREATIVE PAPERBACKS
International copyright reserved in all countries. No part of this book may be reproduced in any form without written permission from the publisher.

DESIGN AND PRODUCTION
by Joe Kahnke; art direction by Rita Marshall
Printed in China

PHOTOGRAPHS by Creative Commons Wikimedia (Paulmcdonald), Dreamstime (Cjh Photography Llc), Getty Images (GraphicaArtis, Photo by Mike Kline [notkalvin]/Moment, Pictorial Parade, Oscar White/Corbis/VCG), iStockphoto (benkrut, JByard), Nic Lehoux, Shutterstock (BATKA, dikobraziy, Jellicle, josep perianes jorba, Ranier Lesniewski, photo.ua, Piotr Przyluski, Alexey Pushkin, Frank Romeo, saraporn)

Image on p. 10 used by permission of the State Historical Society of Missouri: Arthur Witman Photograph Collection, 702.385. The State Historical Society of Missouri.

FIRST EDITION HC 9 8 7 6 5 4 3 2 1
FIRST EDITION PBK 9 8 7 6 5 4 3 2 1